Aloha Elvis

Jerry Hopkins

3565 Harding Avenue
Honolulu, Hawai'i 96816
toll free: (800) 910-2377
phone: (808) 734-7159
fax: (808) 732-3627
e-mail: sales@besspress.com
www.besspress.com

Design: Carol Colbath

Cover photo courtesy of Bob Klein Archives

Library of Congress Cataloging-in-Publication Data

Hopkins, Jerry.
   Aloha Elvis / Jerry Hopkins.
         p.   cm.
   Includes illustrations.
   ISBN 10: 1-57306-273-1
   ISBN 13: 978-1-57306-273-2
   1. Presley, Elvis, 1933-1977.
2. Hawaii—In motion pictures.
3. Hawaii—Description and travel.
4. Music—Hawaii—History and
criticism. I. Title.
ML420.P96.H67 2007 782.421—dc21

Printed in China

CONTENTS

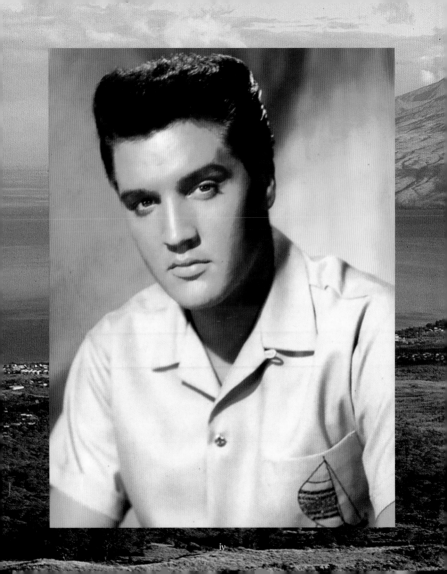

iy

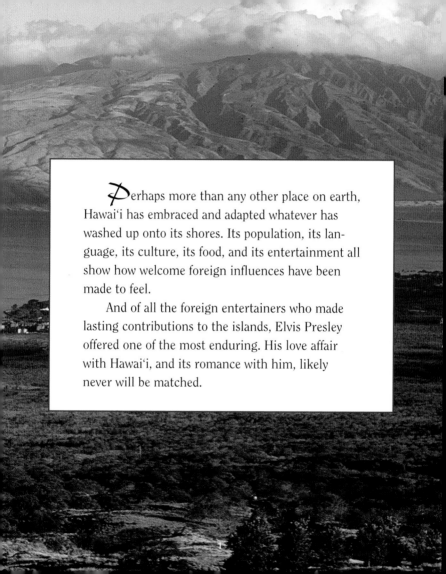

Perhaps more than any other place on earth, Hawai'i has embraced and adapted whatever has washed up onto its shores. Its population, its language, its culture, its food, and its entertainment all show how welcome foreign influences have been made to feel.

And of all the foreign entertainers who made lasting contributions to the islands, Elvis Presley offered one of the most enduring. His love affair with Hawai'i, and its romance with him, likely never will be matched.

THE HAOLES SING AND DANCE, TOO

The impact of the foreigner in Hawai'i's history is much argued. Did what came to be called the *haole* do harm or good? The answer, clearly, is both.

Yet it can also be argued that no area of enterprise offered more pleasure and effect than that offered by foreign musicians and entertainers.

Before what the white man boldly calls "discovery"—meaning his—Hawai'i's music and dance were all simplicity. Musical instruments were primitive, the chants monotonous (mono-tonal). This is not to denigrate the *mele* and hula. There was a link to the ancient gods, the emotion was genuine, there was even a bit of choreography. But taking a world view, they could fairly be said to be limited.

But this was to change dramatically.

*C*alvinist missionaries from New England arrived from the 1820s onward, and with the ancient *kapu* system recently dismantled, several Hawaiian chiefs converted to Christianity. As Gavan Daws noted in *Shoal of Time*, "The natives understood that their old gods had abdicated in favor of a single new god with a new set of kapus." Among them: the banning of the "heathenish" hula.

At the same time, the missionaries brought with them a new music, the hymns, or *hīmeni*, that accompanied and espoused Christianity's stories and messages. Thus was introduced a range of vocal and ensemble singing that moved ancient island *mele* and chant into the modern world. Where melody and harmony were scarcely known—despite the obvious skill and art—now they took a lead role, accompanied by musical instruments that already had shaped music worldwide.

These were the piano and the organ, so key to the singing of hymns, carried by ship from New England around the tip of South America to Polynesia, now to accompany choirs of Hawaiian voice.

$\mathcal{T}$wo more instruments from the western world made an appearance.

In 1878, Portuguese field workers imported to work in the sugar cane fields brought with them the four-stringed *braguinha*, the small fiddle-like instrument that became the *'ukulele*, or "jumping flea" that the fast-moving fingers were said to resemble. (That's one story, anyway.) It quickly was adapted by Hawaiian hands, offering a sprightly sound to the standard island ensemble.

No one is sure when the guitar appeared, but it got a boost when the paniolos, or Hawaiian cowboys, brought it to Big Island ranches in 1832. Although Henry Berger didn't allow the instrument in the Royal Hawaiian Band, which he conducted in the late 19th century, it later became an essential island sound as well, especially when the strings were "slackened."

When
HILO
HATTIE
does the Hilo Hop
by
DON McDIARMID
and JOHNNY NOBLE

YAAKA HULA HICKEY DULA
(HAWAIIAN LOVE SONG)

Successfully
Introduced
AL JOLSON
in
ROBINSON CRUSOE, JR.
Winter Garden
NEW YORK

BY
E. RAY GOETZ
JOE YOUNG &
PETE WENDLING

THEY'RE WEARING 'EM
HIGHER IN HAWAII

E. GOODWIN

HALSEY K. MOHR

O'BRIEN IS TRYIN' TO LEARN
TO TALK HAWAIIAN

NOVELTY
SONG

WORDS BY
AL DUBIN
MUSIC BY
RENNIE CORMACK

M. WITMARK & SONS

The hula survived, of course, going underground and then reemerging in the last years of the monarchy when King Kalākaua gave it his blessing and support and when Hawaiian performers took their music and dance to the United States, building the first audience outside the islands. A "Hawaiian craze" swept across much of the western world in the early 1900s, when steel guitars and hula dancers from the islands became staples on the vaudeville and music hall circuits in the United States and England.

Tin Pan Alley, the collective of composers and publishers that dominated America's popular music for the first half of the century, responded by producing such songs as "They're Wearing 'Em Higher in Hawaii" (the grass skirts—get it?), "O'Brien Is Tryin' to Learn to Talk Hawaiian," and "Oh, How She Could Yacki Hacki Wicki Woo." Another song using gibberish as Hawaiian, "Yaaka Hula Hickey Dula," was a big hit for Al Jolson. Most of the composers of these songs resided in New York and had never been to Hawai'i, but their impact on what followed was undeniable.

PRINCESS POO-POO'-LY
HAS PLENTY PA-PA'-YA
(And she Loves to Give it Away)
WORDS AND MUSIC BY Harry Owens
ORIGINAL IDEA SUGGESTED BY DOUG REYNOLDS
LA SALLE
The
PHONOGRAPH RECORD
SENSATION OF THE YEAR
Recorded by
HARRY OWENS
AND HIS ROYAL HAWAIIANS
ON DECCA No. 2931
OTHER RECORDS BY
ABE LYMAN • GEORGE OLSEN
FREDDIE MARTIN • DICK JURGENS
ROYAL MUSIC PUBLISHER
3502 LARGA AVENUE • LOS ANGELES, CALIF.
P. O. BOX 1756 • HONOLULU, HAWAII

*I*n Hawaiian music today, there is a genre called *hapa haole*, meaning "half Hawaiian," the presumption being that there is a mixture of Hawaiian and Caucasian influences. The term is used to describe a song that has predominantly English lyrics interspersed with one or more Hawaiian words. The instrumentation likely is Hawaiian, but not exclusively, and the song's subject surely will be, but the tune's structure and "sound" are western.

More often than not, the songs were composed by *haole* who lived in Hawai'i. Good examples are the romantic "Beyond the Reef" (which contains neither Hawaiian words nor any mention of Hawai'i directly), "Keep Your Eyes on the Hands" (a song about the hula, obviously), "My Little Grass Shack (in Kealakekua, Hawaii)," and the humorous "Princess Poo-Pooly Has Plenty Pa-Pa-Ya" (the fruit a reference to a buxom woman's breasts).

*I*t was no surprise when Hollywood discovered the islands, making them a favorite location for motion pictures. Some were of a historical nature (*From Here to Eternity*), others more hysterical (would you believe Shirley Temple, Ma Kettle, and Minnie Mouse doing the hula?), some more musical than theatrical (Bing Crosby in *Waikiki Wedding*; "Sweet Leilani" won the Oscar for the best song), others merely here for the scenery (*Gidget Goes Hawaiian*).

Virtually all of them called attention to the music in at least a scene or two, thus advancing the islands' reputation as a sensual, carefree, musical place.

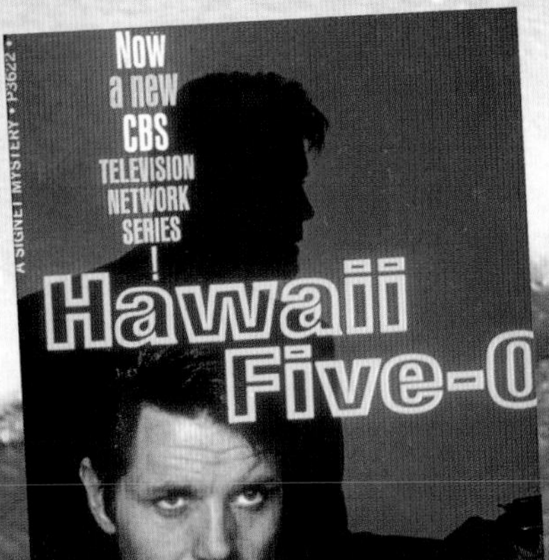
A SIGNET MYSTERY • P3622 •
Now
a new
CBS
TELEVISION
NETWORK
SERIES
!
Hawaii
Five-O
STARRING
Jack Lord as
Steve McGarrett
and James McArthur
as Danny Williams

*R*adio and television brought still more attention to the islands.

More than 300 Hawaiian musicians and singers appeared on the radio show *Hawaii Calls* during its forty years on the air, first beamed to the West Coast via shortwave and later broadcast around the world. Hosted by Webley Edwards, it openly promoted the islands as a tourist destination, beginning each show with the sound of the waves on Waikīkī Beach. A series of *Hawaii Calls* long-play record albums followed.

Television came, too, most remarkably with *Adventures in Paradise* and, later, Jack Lord's long run in *Hawaii Five-0* and Tom Selleck's romp, *Magnum P.I.* Once again, the focus was on the scenery. Back in the 1950s, Arthur Godfrey televised several specials from Hawai'i and regularly used Hawaiian musicians on his variety series for CBS TV. Other television shows followed, hosted by Don Ho.

Thus, every form of modern communication from outside—stage and screen, radio and TV, recordings—influenced Hawai'i's song and dance.

Then came the King of Rock and Roll, Elvis Presley. Like a "clean-up" hitter in a baseball game, with men on all the bases, Elvis stepped up to the plate.

THE KING'S CORONATION, 1957

It began inauspiciously, as two shows tacked onto the end of a mainland tour in October 1957. The tour promoter said Hawai'i didn't have the population to warrant two shows, even if Elvis was then the most popular recording artist in the United States, perhaps everywhere; "Teddy Bear" had gone to No. 1 worldwide that summer and "Jailhouse Rock" was released shortly before the concert dates.

Elvis's manager, Colonel Tom Parker, insisted. The Colonel knew something that the promoter didn't: Elvis received some 21,000 Christmas cards from Hawai'i fans the previous year—an astonishing number, given the Territory's relatively modest population of 600,000.

21,000 Isle Christmas Cards in '56 Gave Elvis Idea to Sing Here Sunday

Elvis Presley's manager, Colonel Tom Parker, said today the biggest incentive for the rock 'n roll singer's appearance here were the 21,000 Christmas cards received from Hawaiian Island fans last year.

The gyrating Presley is scheduled to perform in two shows, 3 and 8:15 p.m., Sunday in the Honolulu Stadium.

He arrives on the Matsonia scheduled to dock at 9 a.m. Saturday and will probably take the next ship back to Los Angeles and on to Memphis, Tennessee, according to Parker.

"The boy hates air[...]

day" and two days later he was here making arrangements.

Original plans for an Australian tour were canceled, "but we may change our minds at the last minute," he said.

Presley, who grosses $800,000 annually, will be assisted on stage by the Blue Moon Boys, a band combo; the Jordannaires quartet, and a variety troupe.

Parker, who has been managing the money-making Presley for more than two years, describes his charge as "a very popular b[...]

$\mathcal{E}$lvis promised his mother he wouldn't fly if he didn't have to, so he took the four-and-a-half-day trip to Hawai'i with a bunch of his buddies on the S.S. *Matsonia*, a cruise liner that in the days before the jumbo jets was one of the favored ways to get to the islands.

On the luxury ship, Elvis befriended O'ahu resident Velma Fisher and babysat her kids, played shuffleboard with his friends and other passengers, posed for pictures, and played the piano in the lounge (convincing one of Velma's young daughters that he'd written "Love Me Tender" just for her).

The arrival in Honolulu was less serene, with thousands of fans waiting at the pier. Elvis's buddies formed a football V-formation to get him through the crowd and into a fleet of limousines that took them to their hotel.

A story not told—and possibly never known to Elvis himself—was the secret that his manager, Colonel Parker, held.

The truth was that Colonel Thomas A. Parker was not an American, as he claimed. His real name was Andreas (Dries) Cornelis van Kujick, and he was Dutch, born in the Netherlands, and an illegal immigrant to the United States. Despite that, he had served in the U.S. Army, serving at Fort DeRussy and then at Fort Shafter in 1929, where his commanding officer was named Thomas R. Parker.

Parker stopped writing letters home, adopted his new name—the "Colonel" was an honorary title bestowed later by the governor of Tennessee—and used it for the rest of his life. His memories of Hawai'i had been pleasant, and one of the reasons he agreed to have Elvis perform here was so he could visit old haunts. More than twenty-five years had passed. Who'd remember?

*R*ock and roll had come to Hawai'i before Elvis, when a disc jockey named Tom Moffatt was the first to play "Rock Around the Clock" by Bill Haley and His Comets in 1955. Rock music didn't kill more traditional Hawaiian music, but you could fairly call it seriously wounded.

When Elvis arrived, Moffatt was spinning records for KHVH, a station atop the new Hilton Hawaiian Village Hotel. This was also where Elvis and his entourage of buddies and the Colonel stayed, taking the entire floor below the radio station. Uncle Tom and his program manager, Ron Jacobs, couldn't have been more pleased. For most of the weekend Tom played only Elvis's records, and on Saturday, Ron put the station engineer in a wig and drove him around the island, saying it was Elvis and causing chaos when they disrupted football halftime ceremonies at Honolulu Stadium.

The Colonel told Uncle Tom and his sidekick it was a good stunt, asking them to emcee the shows the next day. After that, Uncle Tom had an inside track with Elvis.

*N*ext day, Elvis and his trio of musicians took the stage at Honolulu Stadium. It was just a boxing ring with a sound system that Uncle Tom described as "pretty much what they used for boxing and the lights were the ring lights overhead, but that didn't matter with the raw excitement projected by Elvis.

"One thing I will never forget was his encore number. He had just done 'Hound Dog,' started to go off the stage, and of course the crowd went crazy. So, he came back and did this slow, sexy version of 'Hound Dog.'

"He jumped off the stage and sang to the audience. And the barriers were nothing like they are today, just a piece of fencing. So you could see Elvis through the fencing, and he was down on his knees singing. Then he was swept away in a limo . . . ."

Wahiawa citizens

★★★★★★★★★★★★★★★★★★★★★★★★

ONE DAY ONLY

IN PERSON

(Mr. Dynamite)

NEXT SUNDAY
NOVEMBER 10

★ ELVIS
PRESLEY

PLUS A COMPLETE SHOW

HONOLULU STADIUM
2 SHOWS
3:00 P.M. and 8:15 P.M.
RESERVED SEATS $2.50 and $3.50
UNRESERVED $1.50
Including Tax

★★★★★★★★★★★★★★★★★★★★★★

TICKET SALE OPENS 8:45 A.M. TODAY AT:

HONOLULU STADIUM
Phone 95251 for information

THAYER PIANO CO.
116 So. Hotel St.

★★★★★★★★★★★★★★★★★★★★★★★★

ELVIS REMEMBERS PEARL HARBOR

Hawai'i made an impression on Elvis. "I will never forget the day the ship pulled out [following the 1957 concert], what a good feeling I had," he said in the only interview he gave—to Uncle Tom—when he was in the army a couple of years later. "It was a wonderful feeling I will never forget. It, ah, when I left Hawai'i, everybody was throwing leis in the water, you know? And everybody was singing 'Aloha' and all that. It was really a nice feeling and I certainly hope to come back again some day, I really do."

$\mathcal{T}$he Colonel did some test marketing in Honolulu. He told Uncle Tom and Ron Jacobs, who now were anchoring Honolulu's first 24-hour rock station, K-POI, that if they could get enough signatures to fill a large roll of blank paper from one of the station's teletype machines, he would see that it was delivered to Elvis in Germany and the first concert he performed when he returned to the States would be in the islands.

The fans lined up, providing many more signatures than required.

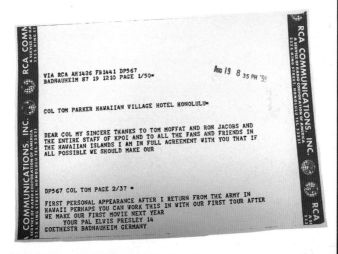

VIA RCA AH1426 FB1441 DP567
BADNAUHEIM 87 19 1210 PAGE 1/50=

AUG 19 8 35 PH '59

COL TOM PARKER HAWAIIAN VILLAGE HOTEL HONOLULU=

DEAR COL MY SINCERE THANKS TO TOM MOFFAT AND RON JACOBS AND
THE ENTIRE STAFF OF KPOI AND TO ALL THE FANS AND FRIENDS IN
THE HAWAIIAN ISLANDS I AM IN FULL AGREEMENT WITH YOU THAT IF
ALL POSSIBLE WE SHOULD MAKE OUR

DP567 COL TOM PAGE 2/37 =

FIRST PERSONAL APPEARANCE AFTER I RETURN FROM THE ARMY IN
HAWAII PERHAPS YOU CAN WORK THIS IN WITH OUR FIRST TOUR AFTER
WE MAKE OUR FIRST MOVIE NEXT YEAR
     YOUR PAL ELVIS PRESLEY 14
GOETHESTR BADNAUHEIM GERMANY

A fund-raising campaign to build a memorial to the men who died during Japan's 1941 attack on Pearl Harbor was floundering. The monument was to be erected at the site of the U.S.S. *Arizona*, where more than a thousand officers and men remained entombed in the sunken battleship beneath harbor waters. An estimated $50,000 was needed to get the project moving again.

When Colonel Parker saw a newspaper story detailing that need, he called the man who'd written it—George Chaplin, editor of the *Honolulu Advertiser*—and volunteered the services of Elvis and his backup band. Thus, Elvis's return to the islands became a charity event.

Three months ahead of the benefit show, the Colonel flew to Hawai'i to hold a press conference, announcing that after the performance, Elvis would remain in the islands to make a movie. In this way, Paramount Pictures would cover many of the Colonel's expenses, at the same time moving events into place that would cement Elvis's role in island history.

*I*n some ways the promotion accompanying the appearance was more subdued than that in 1957. No round-the-clock Elvis marathons occupied the island airwaves. Now, all thirteen O'ahu stations were paid by Elvis to play a half-hour of selections from his first religious album, *His Hand in Mine*, on the first anniversary of his mother's death.

Not quite all was peaceful, of course. When the plane arrived at the airport, Elvis and those traveling with him were held until everyone else got off. Nashville comedian Minnie Pearl, who was to open the show for Elvis, remembered, "There were twenty-five hundred screaming women at the airport. Jimmy Stewart [who was on the same flight] got off and they didn't even recognize him."

A press conference followed at the hotel—
attended by "reporters" from nearly a hundred O'ahu
high schools and middle schools, along with the local
press—and then everyone rushed to the navy base's
four-thousand-seat Bloch Arena for the evening concert.

Honolulu Advertiser columnist Eddie Sherman
was enlisted to help sell Elvis photographs to the fans.
"The Colonel says to me, 'I'll sell 'em, you collect the
money, and whatever they give you, one dollar, five
dollars, ten dollars, don't give 'em any change.'"

1. HEART BREAK HOTEL

2. ALL SHOOK UP
3. FOOL SUCH AS I
4. I GOT A WOMAN
5. LOVE ME ———— INTRODUCE THE B
6. SUCH A NIGHT
7. RECONSIDER BABY
8. I NEED YOUR LOVE TONIGHT
9. THAT'S ALL RIGHT
10. ~~DOING THE BEST I CAN~~
    DON'T BE CRUEL
11. ONE NIGHT
12. ARE YOU LONESOME TONIGHT
13. NOW OR NEVER
14. SWING DOWN
15. HOUND DOG

Larry
These are the songs
we did in show

E. P.

Elvis came out wearing a gold lamé jacket with silver-sequined lapels and cuffs, thumping on a guitar inlaid with mother-of-pearl. There were only fifteen tunes played (as shown here on the song list Elvis gave his musicians), but that seemed to be more than enough.

The local press later talked about a "crackerjack show" and a "boffo extravaganza," and many adults said they couldn't hear anything for the screams, but Peter Guralnick wrote in his biography *Careless Love: The Unmaking of Elvis Presley*, "Even with the poorest home recorder–quality sound, you have only to listen to the tape of the performance that has survived to sense the energy that was coming off the stage, to get a whiff of the ferocity of feeling that the music unleashed . . . [T]here is a sheer joyousness, a guttural exuberance of expression that refuses to be denied."

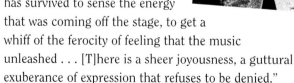

It was also the last time Elvis sang publicly for eight years.

GONE BUT NOT FORGOTTEN.
FROM ELVIS & THE COLONEL

USS ARIZONA

*F*rom the first chords of "Heartbreak Hotel" in 1956, Elvis had Hawai'i's young in his fist. With his *Arizona* performance, he added the new state's adults.

Ticket sales totaled $47,000, to which Elvis and the Colonel added another $5,000—small sums, perhaps, today, but big money in 1961—pushing the benefit over the concert goal. The concert also was credited with helping revive national public sentiment for the Memorial. That September, Congress was prodded into allocating $150,000, and then the Hawai'i legislature added $50,000 to a previous contribution of the same amount. With $250,000 more in federal and state funds and $275,000 in public contributions, the Memorial was completed.

$\mathcal{F}$ollowing the concert, Elvis went right into the filming of *Blue Hawaii*, his eighth movie in just five years. Rarely has a performer been so prolific.

One result was that by now, his films were so individualized, they were a category unto themselves—like Jerry Lewis movies, or the Bing Crosby–Bob Hope "road" movies—most of them appearing to be little more than an excuse to get the singer into a recording studio to produce another soundtrack album. Add some pretty young women and scenery and, voilà! You have an Elvis Presley movie.

In time, Elvis would make three a year, one for each school holiday: spring break, summer, and Christmas.

BLUE HAWAII

Blue Hawaii didn't offer much. Elvis played a young man returning to the islands following two years in the army and determined not to join his father in the pineapple business. Instead, he took a job with a travel agency, where his *hapa haole* girlfriend, played by Joan Blackman, worked.

There followed the predictable lineup of scenes, where Elvis argued with his father, got into a fight at a luau, went to jail, lost his job, and in the end started his own agency, convincing his dad to use him to plan the pineapple company's next convention. Along the way, there were romantic misunderstandings, and as noted on the movie poster, fourteen opportunities to sing.

$\mathcal{S}$till, the movie had beauty and charm. Elvis was Elvis, after all, and the settings could not be faulted.

In fact, the outstanding performances in *Blue Hawaii* may have been those played by Hawai'i's luscious scenery—with stops at Waikīkī Beach, the Ala Wai Yacht Harbor, Punchbowl, Ala Moana Park, Hanauma Bay, Tantalus, and the Waioli Tea Room on O'ahu; and Anahola, Lydgate Park, and the Wailua River on Kaua'i (which Elvis pronounced COW-EYE).

It almost seemed as if someone had been told to bring Hawai'i's best postcards to life.

Some of the music was good, too. The material included some of the filler associated with his earlier, and later, movies, but there also was the film's title tune, "Blue Hawaii," previously recorded by Bing Crosby in 1937 for another motion picture for Paramount, *Waikiki Wedding*, a song famed for a refrain that delivers Hawai'i's quintessential promise: "Dreams come true/in blue Hawaii."

Another classic worked into the story line was "Aloha 'Oe," the poignant farewell that was one of the best known of all Hawaiian melodies, written by Hawai'i's last queen, Lili'uokalani, and a staple in every island vocalist's repertoire.

A third was "Ke Kali Nei Au," better known as "The Hawaiian Wedding Song." Written by Charles E. King, one of Hawai'i's most revered composers, it was always performed as a duet by lovers, as it was at a nightly dinner show at the Coco Palms Hotel on Kaua'i, where many of the film's scenes were shot.

Finally, Elvis sang "Can't Help Falling in Love [With You]," a song that became his dramatic show-closer years later when he returned to live performances.

Blue Hawaii also marked Elvis's first real introduction to the islands. When appearing in concert, he saw little more than the inside of hotel rooms and limousines. Now he had time to look around, and he took to the place if not like a native, at least like a man who enjoyed the soft tropical climate and Hawai'i's relaxed way of life.

Part of what made the movie attractive was that Elvis genuinely appeared to be enjoying himself—because, his friends said, he was.

Hawai'i wasn't a second home for him yet, but the early signs were clear.

RCA VICTOR

PRESENTS
AN ORIGINAL SOUND TRACK ALBUM
14 GREAT SONGS

SEE
ELVIS
IN HAL WALLIS'

**BLUE
HAWAII**

14 GREAT

LPM-2426

Blue Hawaii

Words and Music by LEO ROBIN and RALPH RAINGER

**Elvis
Presley**

Best Wishes
Elvis Presley

FAMOUS MUSIC CORPORATION

Blue Hawaii was a huge success for Elvis. It was one of the top-grossing films of the year, and the soundtrack album was one of the best sellers for both 1961 and 1962. And in time, it would bring him back to the islands to make two more films.

In the long history of movies made in Hawai'i, it also remains one of the true classics. More than forty years later, it frequently appears on television, and in 2001 it was used by the City of Honolulu to open an every-weekend program of films shown on a big screen erected on Waikīkī Beach.

Not only the fans liked it. The Hawaii Visitors Bureau surely must be eternally grateful.

13 of The Coolest Songs in RCA'S Fabulous "Girls! Girls! Girls!" Album!

ELVIS PRESLEY HAL WALLIS' PRODUCTION "GIRLS! GIRLS! GIRLS!" TECHNICOLOR

STELLA STEVENS · JEREMY SLATE · LAUREL GOODWIN

62/377

GIRLS! GIRLS! GIRLS!

A year later, with the sweet smell of the success of *Blue Hawaii* still as fresh, and alluring, as that of Hawai'i's aromatic *pīkake*, ginger, and plumeria, Elvis returned to the islands with many from his earlier crew, hoping to strike gold again.

Sadly, it didn't work. He had the same producer and director and the usual backup cast of seasoned actors and attractive young females, but the film with what appeared to be a computer-generated title—*Girls! Girls! Girls!*—was cinematic junk food. The ingredients seemed to be there, but it was all empty calories.

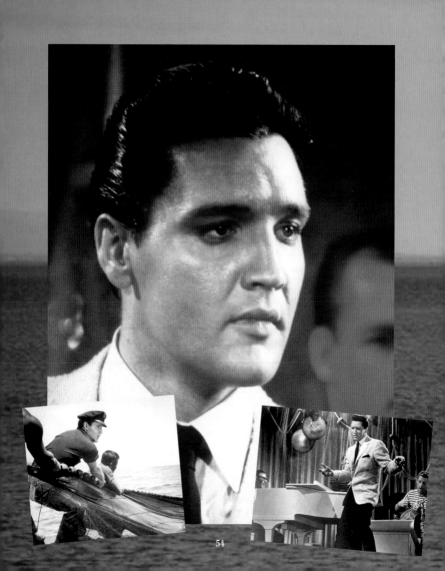

$\mathcal{T}$his time Elvis played the skipper of a charter fishing boat who worked for a man who also owned a sleek sailboat that had been built by Elvis's father. Elvis wanted to buy the craft, but the owner was forced to sell it to a broker, who then doubled its price. Elvis went to work on one of the broker's shrimp boats and took a second job singing in the club where Stella Stevens worked. Stevens was in love with Elvis, but he was in love with Laurel Goodwin, who bought the boat for him. Elvis felt shamed by the charity and he fled to Paradise Cove. Goodwin followed and Elvis asked her to marry him.

What was missing was Hawai'i. There were plenty of scenes shot at sea and there was an obligatory beach scene (with Tahitian dancers), but the postcards were gone and a fishing charter, shrimp boat, and night club—the three primary sets—could have been found anywhere.

*H*awai'i was left out of the music, too.

Shrimp fishing has never been a big thing in Hawai'i, but that was how the script read, and the tunesmiths-for-hire followed right along, thus "Song of the Shrimp" and "We're Coming in Loaded."

Of the thirteen cuts on the soundtrack album that was marketed along with the film—just in time for year-end holiday moviegoers in 1962— only one deserved real praise. This was "Return to Sender," written by Otis Blackwell, a rhythm-and-blues singer who had also written "Don't Be Cruel" and "All Shook Up," two of Elvis's big early hits. It, too, was in the novelty ballad vein, with the letter serving as a metaphor for unrequited love.

Even the title song, composed by Jerry Leiber and Mike Stoller, who wrote "Hound Dog" and "Jailhouse Rock," failed to repeat their earlier success.

PARADISE, HAWAIIAN STYLE

In 1966, Elvis returned for his third and final
island motion picture.

Elvis was still making his formula films and he
was rich now, earning as much as $750,000 for each
movie, plus 50 percent of the profits—another seem-
ingly small sum nowadays, but large for the time;
soon Elvis would be one of the first to be paid a mil-
lion dollars for a picture.

The times had changed, too. The world was a
more serious place. Bob Dylan and the Beatles had
captured the music market. There were civil rights
marches and protests against the war in Vietnam.
John Kennedy had been assassinated. Nothing was the
same after that.

However archaic Elvis may have seemed in com-
parison, the Colonel figured that when you had a
successful formula, you didn't tinker with it. Thus,
Paradise, Hawaiian Style.

Of the three movies, *Paradise, Hawaiian Style*
had the thinnest and most preposterous plot. Now
Elvis was a pilot who suggested a partnership in a hel-
icopter tour company with a friend (played by James
Shigeta, a native of Oʻahu, then establishing his name
in Hollywood). Elvis got into trouble when he nearly
crashed into a car driven by a
Federal Aviation Agency officer,
who reacted by suspending the
pilot's license. More problems
involved a company secretary who
rejected Elvis and the Shigeta
character's daughter, who caused
the two men to fight. Then, when
Shigeta crashed, Elvis flew off to
rescue him, telling the FAA he
violated his suspension only to
save his friend. He and Shigeta shook hands and the
Girl Friday decided she liked Elvis after all.

That was another thing you could count on in an
Elvis movie: a happy ending.

$\mathcal{T}$he music was anemic again, too. Save for some interesting Polynesian pageantry—about which, more in a moment—the soundtrack album that predictably accompanied the movie to the marketplace did little to stir any but the most ardent Elvis fans.

Once again, Elvis was given a handful of novelty songs. Elvis sang similar melodies in most of his films and much of the criticism they attracted came because the music seemed diluted, the lyrics sappy and trivial, compared with the depth of emotion and force displayed in his earlier rock (and religious) performances.

Still, the genre was legitimate, however inconsequential—remember all the *hapa haole* songs about little grass shacks and the hula?—and in that context, a critic should only ask: were the songs in *Paradise, Hawaiian Style* worthy, musically? Not even the Colonel could find one he wanted to release as a single.

$\mathcal{W}$hat saved the film was Hawai'i. Not only had Elvis returned to the islands to make the film, but as in *Blue Hawaii*, Hawai'i was written back into the film.

In large part, this was accomplished by shooting several scenes at the Polynesian Cultural Center, a popular tourist attraction on O'ahu's windward side. Here, Brigham Young University students—many from all over the Pacific—worked part-time in the Center to earn tuition credit, serving meals, demonstrating traditional island crafts, and wearing costumes in highly commercialized but generally authentic pageants of song and dance, some of which were incorporated into the script.

The use of so many "local" extras—plus the featured roles filled by Shigeta and nine-year-old Donna Butterworth, who played his daughter—added more authenticity to the movie.

Paradise, Hawaiian Style fared little better at the box office or in the record stores than the previous film, but Elvis sank deeper personal roots in the islands during the filming, connections that continued for years to come.

One of Elvis's buddies married a Brigham Young University student, and her return to the mainland with her husband served as a reminder to Elvis and others in his family of the beauty of Hawaiʻi left behind.

Many things, large and small, in time conspired to make Hawaiʻi a holiday destination. Two years later, in 1968, when Elvis returned with his wife Priscilla, he formed a lasting friendship with Ed Parker, a part-Hawaiian native of Kalihi who operated a school in Los Angeles but was appearing at a karate championship in Honolulu. Through his instruction, Elvis incorporated karate moves and poses in his "comeback" show on NBC TV in 1969 and later when he appeared in Las Vegas and began to tour again.

ALOHA BY SATELLITE

The Colonel was known for staging colossal events—or making small ones seem larger than they were—and the idea he announced in 1972 was one of the biggest, a concert to be broadcast worldwide by satellite from the Honolulu International Center (since renamed the Neal Blaisdell Center), in January 1973.

The show would begin after midnight, Hawai'i time, to allow the live performance to be viewed throughout the Pacific and Asia. The next night the show would be shown in twenty-eight European countries via a Eurovision simulcast, and NBC TV would air the concert in the United States. Ultimately, the Colonel said, Elvis would be seen by half a billion people.

At a press conference it was said that the show, called "Aloha from Hawaii," not only would command history's largest audience, but for the first time an album would be released within days of the performance, an attempt to capitalize on the widespread exposure and to keep the inevitable bootlegged recordings at a minimum.

$\mathcal{N}$o admission could be charged for entertainment broadcast on public airwaves, so when the Colonel received a letter from Eddie Sherman, who had helped sell Elvis photos at the Pearl Harbor show and still was a columnist for the *Honolulu Advertiser*, and Sherman proposed the concert be turned into another charity event, the singer's manager agreed.

This time the beneficiary was the Kui Lee Cancer Fund, named for the beloved Hawai'i composer and singer who died at age thirty-four in 1964. Elvis included one of Kui's songs, "I'll Remember You," on an album released that year, and it was agreed that contributions would be accepted at both the dress rehearsal and the televised show.

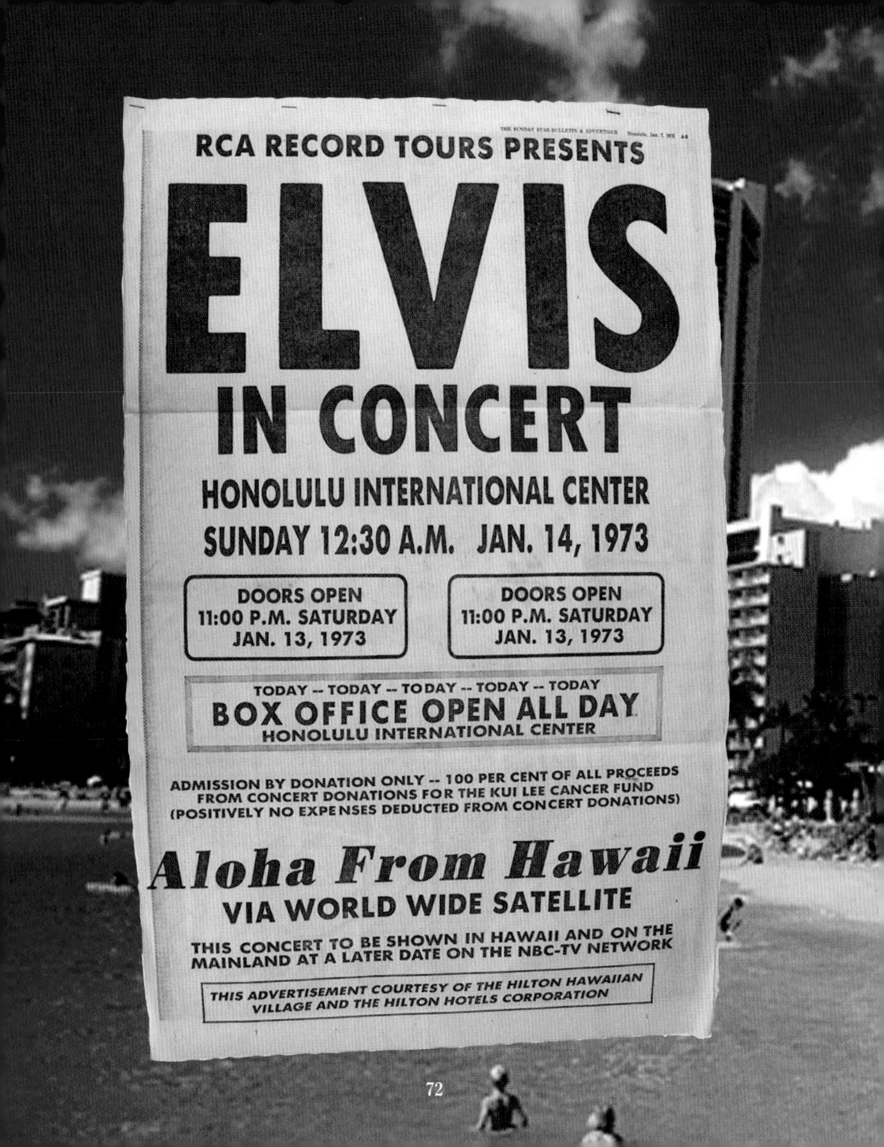

THE SUNDAY STAR-BULLETIN & ADVERTISER Honolulu, Jan. 7

RCA RECORD TOURS PRESENTS

ELVIS
IN CONCERT

HONOLULU INTERNATIONAL CENTER

SUNDAY 12:30 A.M. JAN. 14, 1973

DOORS OPEN
11:00 P.M. SATURDAY
JAN. 13, 1973

DOORS OPEN
11:00 P.M. SATURDAY
JAN. 13, 1973

TODAY -- TODAY -- TODAY -- TODAY -- TODAY
BOX OFFICE OPEN ALL DAY
HONOLULU INTERNATIONAL CENTER

ADMISSION BY DONATION ONLY -- 100 PER CENT OF ALL PROCEEDS FROM CONCERT DONATIONS FOR THE KUI LEE CANCER FUND (POSITIVELY NO EXPENSES DEDUCTED FROM CONCERT DONATIONS)

Aloha From Hawaii

VIA WORLD WIDE SATELLITE

THIS CONCERT TO BE SHOWN IN HAWAII AND ON THE MAINLAND AT A LATER DATE ON THE NBC-TV NETWORK

THIS ADVERTISEMENT COURTESY OF THE HILTON HAWAIIAN VILLAGE AND THE HILTON HOTELS CORPORATION

$\mathcal{T}$he plan was to recreate for the rest of the world the show that Elvis had been performing in Las Vegas and in tours across the United States.

The cast was large, including the Joe Guercio Orchestra and backup singers, the Sweet Inspirations, who had worked for years behind Elvis; J. D. Sumner and the Stamps, a gospel quartet whose leader was such an influence on Elvis when he was growing up in Memphis; and Kathy Westmoreland, whose high soprano was so much a part of his concert sound. Once again, everyone stayed at the Hilton Hawaiian Village Hotel, rehearsals being held in the Hilton Dome.

For the Honolulu media, Elvis became a daily story. Vegas treated all celebrities as ho-hum, as commonplace in that desert city as heat and neon, and when he was touring Elvis was usually in one place for no longer than it took to sleep for a few hours and do a concert, leaving the next morning before the papers appeared. In Hawai'i, he had a chance to read some of his press—and it contained nothing but the cheeriest praise. Honolulu's mayor Frank Fasi even declared the day of the broadcast "Elvis Presley Day."

$\mathcal{A}$ problem arose when Elvis gave the jeweled belt to his costume to actor Jack Lord. The costume designer, who was in Los Angeles, was told to make another, fast. "But we've used the last of the rubies!" he cried. "We'll have to get more from Europe!"

On the evening of the show there were technical problems, caused when the engineers flown in from Hollywood to record the show brought so much electrical equipment, they exhausted the local power source, and two hours before going on the air they picked up a hum from the lights.

"We thought we'd lose the album and had to go scrounging to the Navy to borrow thick lead sheets to baffle the hum," the producer said. "They came in, sirens blaring from Pearl Harbor, and we got them in place just minutes before we started broadcasting."

$\mathcal{E}$lvis sang twenty-two songs, a selection that swept up some of his distant past ("Love Me," "Blue Suede Shoes," "Long Tall Sally," "Johnny B. Goode," and "Hound Dog"), mixed deftly with newer material ("American Trilogy," "You Gave Me a Mountain," "Burning Love," "Suspicious Minds"), and a song that Frank Sinatra more or less made his own, "My Way," though it could be argued that Elvis had gone his own way, too. Plus, of course, Kui Lee's "I'll Remember You" and Elvis's local theme song, "Blue Hawaii."

Conforming to patterns long established, Elvis leaned down into the audience so fans could encircle his neck with hugs and leis. Behind him, signs saying "We Love Elvis" blinked and flashed in a dozen languages.

As he finished his traditional closing song, "Can't Help Falling in Love," he dropped to one knee, right fist raised in triumph, his head bowed in simultaneous humility. He stood. His jeweled cape was draped on his shoulders. Elvis's head remained bowed for a moment, and then he took the $10,000 cape and sailed it into the audience like a Frisbee. Throwing up a hand in the Hawaiian shaka sign, he finally left the stage.

Although the show cost approximately $2.5 million to produce, the most spent on any entertainment special to date, it was regarded as a huge success. The Colonel characteristically claimed that Elvis attracted a billion viewers—a boast impossible to prove or disprove—and when the program was aired on NBC it won a 57 percent share of those watching television and earned generally good reviews.

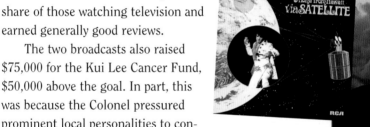

The two broadcasts also raised $75,000 for the Kui Lee Cancer Fund, $50,000 above the goal. In part, this was because the Colonel pressured prominent local personalities to contribute $1,000 apiece to watch the show, while many children got in for a penny.

The Sunday *Advertiser*, active in promoting the show, ran a lead editorial saying, "Elvis Presley continues to be a great, good friend of Hawaii." The newspaper reminded readers that this was the second time that Elvis had "delivered for Hawaii in a big way," recalling the *Arizona* benefit. "In 1973, as in 1961, Elvis and Colonel Parker, who shares his affection for Hawaii, deserve the islands' great thanks and warmest aloha."

HE DID IT HIS WAY

Elvis followed the satellite show with a brief holiday, visiting the Oʻahu home of Jack and Marie Lord, giving the actor a gold-plated revolver and his wife an emerald and diamond ring. Elvis also said that *Hawaii Five-O* was one of his favorite shows and that, in fact, he had every episode on video.

The 1973 satellite concert was Elvis's last performance in Hawaiʻi and, tragically, the last big challenge of his career. Elvis continued to play Vegas and tour, but stopped making the movies where, as he put it, he did little more than "sing to turtles." A couple of documentaries followed, but his failing health was now evident, affecting his performances. He had gone on a crash diet for the satellite show, but the poundage returned. Hospital visits followed.

There were other problems. His divorce from Priscilla—who had left him for a karate instructor she met in Hawaiʻi (not Ed Parker)—turned nasty and by 1976 Elvis's longtime relationship with another woman ended. The money continued to pour in, but if he made as much as an Arabian prince, he spent as much as two.

The end was near.

*H*e leased a house on the beach in Lanikai and took his last vacation there, in March 1977. One evening, he and his friends were sneaked in for the show at the Polynesian Cultural Center. Other times, he went to one of the small shopping centers in Kailua, where he greeted fans warmly, bought gifts for his companions, and on one occasion, paid the bill for a stranger who was making a purchase for his wife.

Kalani Simerson, a onetime Waikīkī performer who operated a successful limousine service and was both friend and driver to Elvis, visited him in Lanikai. "We played football," Kalani said, "and it was sad, very sad. Elvis was overweight and just unable to function normally. I guess it was all that medication they said he took. Somebody'd throw him the ball and he'd catch it and start running and he couldn't stop. He just wasn't able to control his own body. One time he ran right into a cyclone fence."

Various illnesses, his lifelong poor diet, and an addiction to prescription drugs inevitably took their toll.

$\mathcal{E}$lvis Aron Presley died at his Memphis home five months later, on August 16, 1977. He was 42 years of age.

*I*t doesn't take much of an excuse to run a newspaper story about Elvis Presley today. Elvis is remembered worldwide and even the flimsiest reason, even if imagined, seems to justify a headline.

Yet, in Hawai'i, the memories seem more vivid, more personal, just as they do in Memphis but not in Las Vegas or Los Angeles, where he spent much more time.

Elvis loved Hawai'i," said his longtime friend Tom Moffatt, the disc jockey closest to the Presley-Parker camp over the years, "—from the moment he landed here in 1957, through all his concerts, three movies, and many vacation getaways. And Hawai'i loved Elvis just as much.

"These islands have always been a godsend for celebrities, because people here respect their privacy. Once away from the tourist areas, Elvis could relax and go to the beach just like everyone else."

Thus, Hawai'i was, in a sense, his second home, even in the minds of island residents.

$\mathcal{T}$he commercial connection between Elvis and the islands remains, too.

The old Coco Palms Hotel (now gone) for many years offered a honeymoon package and operated a small museum. Another, larger museum was operated for many years in Waikīkī by another popular singer, Jimmy Velvet, and a store sold Elvis memorabilia at the International Market Place in Waikīkī. Hawai'i license plates with ELVIS in the place of numerals are still a staple souvenir. So, too, a line of Elvis aloha shirts.

There also has been a private home on Pūpūkea where Elvis stayed but once marketed as a vacation rental called "Elvis's Hawaiian Hideaway."

Most impressive is the lineup of Elvis "impersonators" appearing in Waikīkī since the singer's death. Jonathan Von Brana has been the longest-running; Bruno Hernandez, the youngest.

$\mathcal{T}$he most impressive commercial connection of all may be the memorabilia sold at auction and on the Internet.

Promotional items that were distributed freely by the hundreds, if not thousands, to promote the movies now command surprising prices. A paper flower lei promoting *Blue Hawaii* regularly sells at auction for $65, the only thing differentiating it from almost identical leis sold in Waikīkī for under a dollar being a paper medallion, a photo of Elvis in an aloha shirt on one side, a plug for the film on the other.

A more costly souvenir was a blue linen shirt Elvis wore in *Paradise, Hawaiian Style*. A Sotheby's catalog estimated its value at $8,000-$9,000 and it sold for $10,500.

What's the most expensive? It might be one sold by another auction house, one of many items offered by Lisa Marie Presley to benefit a homeless shelter— her father's jeweled cape from the "Aloha from Hawaii" satellite show. Selling price: $85,000!

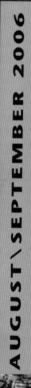

THE OFFICIAL

Elvis Presley

FAN CLUB MAGAZINE

AUGUST\SEPTEMBER 2006

$\mathcal{T}$he connection made by Elvis's enduring fans is also strong.

Charlie Ross surely is the most ardent. She came to the islands from Chicago in 1978 and founded the Elvis Memorial Fan Club—an organization with an international membership, a newsletter, and a determination to get the U.S. Parks Department to give her idol more public credit at the *Arizona* Memorial. She's at elmemh@earthlink.net.

Elvis fans can also click onto http://elvisinhawaii.com, a Web site administered by Martin Nolet in the Netherlands.

For many years, there also have been Elvis tours to O'ahu and Kaua'i, groups coming mainly from the United Kingdom and led by the publisher of *Elvis Monthly* magazine, Todd Slaughter.

$\mathcal{T}$here is a greater tribute to be paid, of course: from the Hawaiian music community.

> "I was born into the music business and had an instinctive awareness of its evolution. Elvis made such an enormous impact on all of our lives, but the true influence was how his music infiltrated Hawaiian music and allowed it to evolve. It actually was the beginning of what we still call the Hawaiian Music Renaissance. Creative musicians incorporated these new sounds into the traditional music and everything changed. Elvis filmed here as well, and his being in Hawai'i just allowed musicians to adopt his rhythms and riffs even further."

> — Jon de Mello, executive producer,
>   The Mountain Apple Company

$\mathcal{F}$or three decades—the 1950s, the 1960s, and the 1970s—Elvis appeared in Hawai'i, either in concert or in films, a record that no other non-Hawaiian performer has likely matched or ever will. His influence and impact were great and surely will be felt for some time.

Elvis was a welcome caller, a generous guest. By giving proceeds from two of his concerts—there were six in all—to prominent and worthy local charities, he won the hearts of all Hawai'i.

His three pretty-as-a-postcard movies boosted the new state's tourism. Some of his most enduring and popular songs came from those movies.

And as was true from the time of the missionaries and migrant laborers, whatever the *haole* brought to the islands—the guitars and western orchestras, the hymns and Hollywood melodies, the electric rock and roll—Hawai'i welcomed and modified, and came to call its own.

PHOTO CREDITS

Covers   Bob Klein Archives.

Endsheets   *Left:* Todd Slaughter Photo Collection. *Middle:* Tom Moffatt Collection. *Right:* Peter Hernandez.

page ii   DeSoto Brown Collection.

page iv   Bob Klein Archives.

page 2   Hawai'i State Archives.

page 6   Bottom *left* and *right*: Hawai'i State Archives.

page 8   DeSoto Brown Collection.

page 10   DeSoto Brown Collection.

page 12   DeSoto Brown Collection.

page 14   *Left:* DeSoto Brown Collection. *Right:* Donna Jung Public Relations.

page 16   Bob Klein Archives.

page 17   *Honolulu Advertiser.*

page 18   With Jana, *left,* and Luana, on the *Matsonia*. Velma Fisher.

page 19   *Honolulu Advertiser.*

page 20   Colonel Parker. Tom Moffatt Collection.

page 22   With Tom Moffatt. Tom Moffatt Collection.

page 24   *Honolulu Advertiser.*

page 25   *Honolulu Advertiser.*

page 26   Bob Klein Archives.

page 27   DeSoto Brown Collection.

page 28   Tom Moffatt, *left,* Colonel Parker, *center,* and Ron Jacobs, *right.* Tom Moffatt Collection.

page 29   Tom Moffatt Collection.

page 30   Hawai'i State Archives.

page 32   Colonel Parker, *left,* and Elvis, *center,* arrive in Honolulu. Julien's Auctions.